I LOVE TO IMAGINE!

Written and illustrated by
Daphne Monique Thomas

I Love to Imagine

ISBN 9781517657178

Printed in the United States of America

I Love to Imagine!

THIS BOOK BELONGS TO

_____

PRESENTED BY

_____

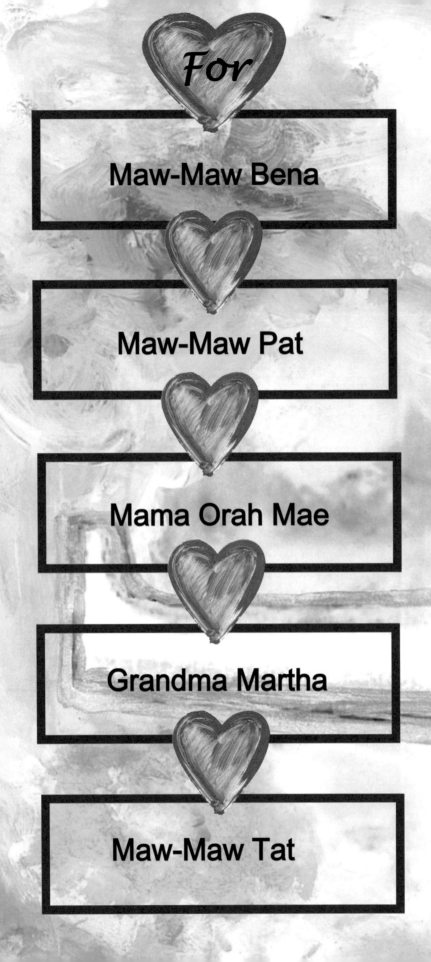

For

Maw-Maw Bena

Maw-Maw Pat

Mama Orah Mae

Grandma Martha

Maw-Maw Tat

Hi, my name is Charli.

That's right,

girls can be

called Charli too!

I just love to imagine...

I think it's fun,

don't you?

Sometimes when

I close my eyes

and sit really,

really still...

I'll use my mind to imagine

that...

I'm climbing up a hill.

I imagine that I'm

climbing,

climbing,

climbing

until I'm up on top,

and then I might imagine…

That I don't want to stop!

My hill has become this huge mountain, that I'm going to climb. Now that I'm done with climbing...

I'll imagine that

I'm flying!

I'm no longer climbing,

but I'm soaring

through the clouds!

I imagine all of the sights I see

down below upon the ground.

I imagine houses that look just

like toys, and tiny cars that go

to and fro,

but now I'm tired of

flying and so...

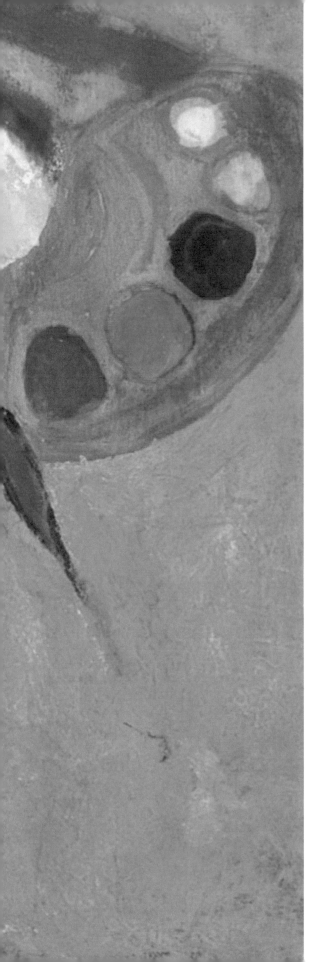

I'll imagine that I'm painting, with a rainbow! The big blue sky will be my canvas because it has lots of room. I'll use red, blue, violet, and green... I'll even use too!

My painting is just so busy. It keeps moving all around. I imagine that these colors can *swirl* and *swirl* and change themselves around!

Now when I imagine,

these colors have a smell…

Not just any

old smell,

but one of my

favorite, favorite

smells!

I imagine that I'm visiting with Grandma, and she's baking in her shiny stove.

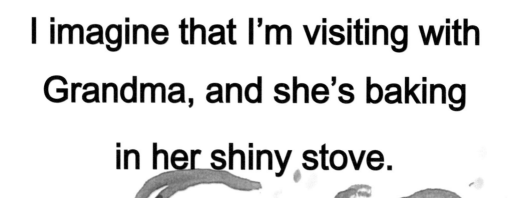

The most wonderful smell fills the room.

... could it be the

chocolate chip

cookies that I just

LOVE?

I'm almost

afraid to open

my eyes what

if the smell

isn't real...

What if it's only my

super

imagination?

You know the one

that wanted to paint

with the rainbow and

climb that hill...

I've got to

take my chances.

I'm going to be **really,**

really, brave...

So here goes…

1-2-3-4-5

I've opened my eyes.

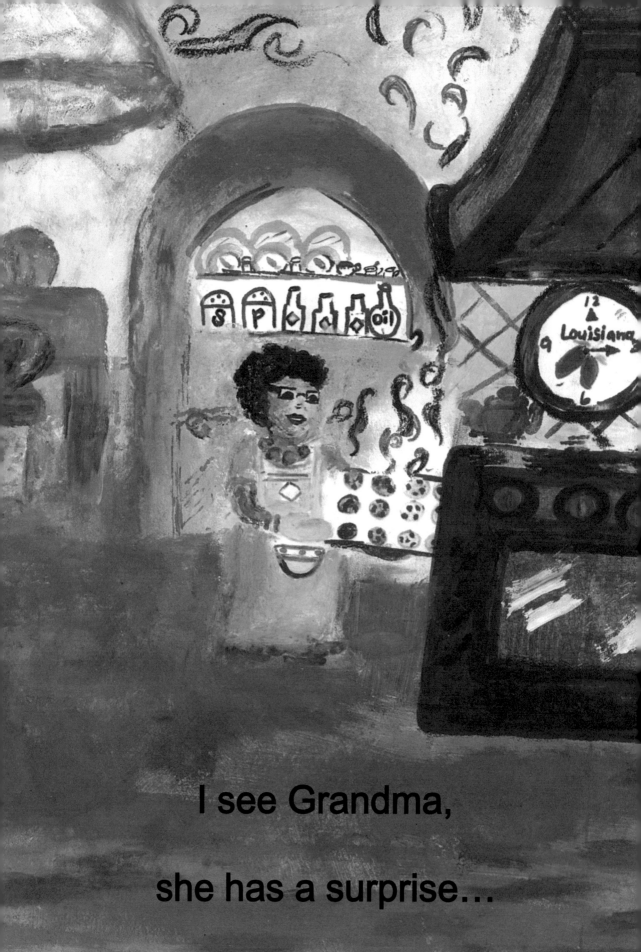

I see Grandma,

she has a surprise…

OHHHH...
Thank you for the cookies!

Make Grandma's Easy to Bake Chocolate Chip Cookies! You'll need:

- 1 stick (1/2 cup) salted butter

- ¾ cup brown sugar

- 1 large egg

- 1 tsp vanilla extract

- 1 ¼ cup flour

- 1 cup chocolate chips

Directions: Ask an adult to preheat the oven to 350 degrees. Next, find a large bowl and a wooden spoon. Pour the sugar and butter in the bowl. Mix the sugar and butter together until they are all mixed together and a little fluffy. Then, crack the egg into the bowl. Mix the egg until it is fully combined. Now it's time to mix in the flour and the yummy chocolate chips. Pour these into the bowl slowly and mix until everything is perfectly bended. Be sure not to mix for too long! Now, take a spoon to scoop out the cookie dough. Each scoop should be placed about two inches apart from each other onto an ungreased baking sheet. Once your baking sheet is full, pop your cookies into the oven for about 8-12 minutes. Have an adult take the cookies out of the oven to cool for about 5 minutes. Then, ENJOY!!!

Now that you have read "I Love to Imagine"... and heard Charli's

point of view. Use these pages along with your creative thinking and

ideas to write your own story. Show and tell exactly what you would

do!

Acknowledgements

With God, ALL things really are possible!

I'd like to thank my husband, Jimmy, for encouraging and supporting my creative vision. Your belief in me and foresight is always reassuring.

I love you!

Thank you to our children Zhamal, Zedric, and Amber for being the beautiful gifts and blessings that you've always been.

I'd like to thank my grandsons, Zedric Jr., and Zayden for whom the grandma character was written!

I love you both more than I can say.

Thank you to my mother, Patricia, who reminded me just before I penned "I love to imagine",

That I fiercely wanted to be a girl named Charli.

Your shared glimpse from my childhood,

literally breathed life into this story! Thanks again Ma!

Happy reading to my great niece who **IS** a lovely girl named Charli!

Thank you to my entire family, each friend, and patron who has listened to these stories for decades when they were mere concepts

To the countless educators that have given their time and expertise to confirm that my works were filled with the academic substance that I hoped they would contain.

"THANK YOU!"

I must thank Mrs. Delores Henderson, a renowned Louisiana storyteller and retired educator for each story that she shared with myself and our clients in my work place...and for recognizing that I had the aptitude to pursue the art form of storytelling that she so loves.

-God Bless!

I also need to thank educator, and dear friend Shannon Bell-woods,

Who heard me express plans to take on this new career path (only upon retirement, which was not in the near future!) and not allowing me to waste an opportunity to get started.

A very special Thank You to Mrs. Savanna Barabin and Mrs. Thelma Phillips former librarians from my beloved Bunche Branch Library. Thank you to Mrs. Barbara Loften Patrick, Mrs. Audrey DePass and Educator Mr. Rodney Tillman Sr. for igniting my artistic flame at the Broussard Harris Recreation Center in Franklin, LA. when I was a child. They are the Art Teachers that instructed me. Thank you to Dr. Karyn Winters for your encouragement and support. From all of you I gained a passion for bridging connections with students, educators, parents and communities.

I am grateful that I've been so blessed!

My hope is to continue to spark a lifelong interest in literature-And to challenge each reader;

To **KNOW**

To **DREAM**

-And to say out loud

" I Love to Imagine!"

.

Made in the USA
Columbia, SC
09 February 2025

52803109R00024